# A "Humbling" of Her

Dedicated to those members of the British Armed Forces who

made a significant contribution to 'Peace' in Northern Ireland

during Operation Banner. 1969 – 2007

Not strictly speaking a collective noun, A 'Humbling' of heroes

is used because I feel very humble to have known, met or even

heard about the people mentioned in this book.

## Introduction.

A "Humbling of Heroes" is my own way of paying my respects to those members of the British Army and the Royal Ulster Constabulary who made a significant contribution to 'Peace' in Northern Ireland. The people mentioned here are merely my selections, based on my personal experiences or events that have had a profound effect on me. Some are well known, others are anonymous. The chapters in this book are not meant to be a comprehensive resume of those mentioned. They are merely the salient facts that I have heard, read or witnessed, or who had a tremendous impact on me. I have the utmost respect for every soldier and policeman who served in Ulster during what has become known as 'The Troubles'. A war that never was. It is not my intention to debate politics or semantics here, nor am I ignoring the civilians on both sides who served or who were killed. I served in Northern Ireland for nearly five years as a soldier and just over a year as a policeman. We soldiers had the utmost respect for the police, after all, when our tour was over, we came home. Most of us anyway. The police, and the Ulster Defence Regiment, lived with the troubles, day in, day out. There is a dispute about exactly how many members of the Armed Forces were killed during those thirty-eight years. The British Government will never publicly recognise the true figure. However, there are many thousands of ex servicemen who will remember those who died in

## Northern Ireland – The Forgotten War.

## Contents

## 1969

1969 will live in my memory for a wide variety of reasons. I was 15 years old in that year and it was the same year that I decided to join the British Army. The Boeing 747 made it's maiden flight, Neil Armstrong, Buzz Aldrin and Michael Collins flew to the Moon with Armstrong being the first human to walk on the planet. The Krays were sent to prison for murder, on the 1st July, Prince Charles, Prince of Wales, was invested at Caernarfon Castle, and, on the 14th August, British Troops were deployed on the streets of Northern Ireland to restore law and order. Initially welcomed, the troops were soon reviled and hated. I salute every member of the British Army, the Ulster Defence Regiment and the Royal Ulster Constabulary who served during Operation Banner, 1969 to 2007.

*"What manner of men are these who wear the maroon red beret? They are firstly all volunteers, and are then toughened by hard physical training. As a result they have that infectious optimism and that offensive eagerness which comes from physical well-being. They have jumped from the air and by doing so have conquered fear. Their duty lies in the van of the battle: they are proud of this honour and have never failed in any task. They have the highest standards in all things, whether it be skill in battle or smartness in the execution of all peace time duties. They have shown themselves to be as tenacious and determined in defence as they are courageous in attack. They are, in fact, men apart - every man an Emperor."*

**Field Marshall The Viscount Montgomery.**

**Sgt Michael Willetts, GC, The Parachute Regiment.**

Square jawed, solidly built with a rugged handsomeness; Michael Willetts was a career soldier, what some people call 'a man's man'. Born in the Midlands town of Sutton-in-Ashfield in August 1943, Willetts left school at 15 and went to work in a colliery. He soon realised that this was not the job for him and so he joined the army and in particular 3rd Battalion The Parachute Regiment. He married Sandra and had two children, Dean and Trudy. Willetts must have been a bloody good soldier because it did not take long for him to reach the rank of Sergeant. In 1971, Willetts and the rest of 3 Para were posted to Belfast on 'Active Service'. He and his squad were based at Springfield Road RUC Station, a station that had already seen plenty of terrorist activity and was to see much more over the coming decades.

On the 25th May 1971, Sgt Willetts was on duty in the inner hall of the Police station when a terrorist entered the reception area carrying a suitcase. Inside this case was a 30lb bomb and the fuse could be seen smoking as it protruded outside the case.

Inside the reception were a man, a woman, two children and several police officers.

Sergeant Willetts received a posthumous George Cross for his actions on that day. The citation for the George Cross reads:

*The Queen has been graciously pleased to approve the posthumous award of the George Cross to Sergeant Michael Willetts, The Parachute Regiment.*

*At 8.24pm on the evening of 25th May 1971, a terrorist entered the reception hall of the Springfield Road Police Station in Belfast. He carried a suitcase from which a smoking fuse protruded, dumped it quickly on the floor and fled outside. Inside were a man and a woman, two children and several police officers. One of the later saw at once the smoking case and raised the alarm. The Police Officers began to organise the evacuation of the hall past the reception desk, through the reception office and out by a door into the rear passage.*

*Sergeant Michael Willetts was on duty in the inner hall. Hearing the alarm, he sent an NCO up to the first floor to warn those above and hastened himself to the door towards which a Police Officer was thrusting those in the reception hall and office. He held the door open while all passed safely through and then stood in the doorway, shielding those taking cover.*

*Sergeant Willetts was mortally wounded. His duty did not require him to enter the threatened area, his post was elsewhere. He knew well, after 4 months service in Belfast, the peril of going towards a terrorist bomb but he did not hesitate to do so. All those approaching the door from the far side agree that if they had had to check to open the door they would have perished. Even when they had reached the rear passage, Sergeant Willetts waited, placing his body as a screen to shelter them. By this considered act of bravery, he risked and lost – his life for those of the adults and children. His selflessness, his courage are beyond praise. 22$^{nd}$ June 1971.*

Other versions state that Sergeant Willetts had realised what was about to happen, thrust the children into a corner and shielded them from the blast. The two children, one of whom was only four years of age, survived the blast thanks to Sergeant Willetts' action.

Whichever is more accurate, the truth is that Sgt Willetts performed an amazing act of valour. How many of us can truthfully say that they would have done the same?

In total, seven RUC officers, two British Soldiers and eighteen civilians were injured in this cowardly, despicable attack. Sgt Willetts was struck in the back of the head by a piece of metal from a metal locker that was thrown across the room by the explosion. He died after two hours on the operating theatre at the Royal Victoria Hospital, Belfast.

# A 'Humbling' of heroes

As Sgt Willetts and the other injured people were being removed by ambulance, a crowd assembled and began to shout, hurling obscenities and insults at the soldiers. It is a true credit to the Parachute Regiment that they continued their patrols and other duties after this outrage without seeking retribution.

Two years later, I was stationed in Regents Park Barracks, London. The Army tasked me to drive a party of nurses from the Royal Victoria Hospital in Belfast who were over in London as a gesture of goodwill and gratitude for their devotion to duty. I collected the nurses from Heathrow Airport and, over the next five days, drove them around the city, showing them the tourist attractions and generally attempting to entertain them. Wherever they wanted to go, I took them and kept a silent watch over them. For the first time in my army career, I was in civilian clothes and armed. My instructions were that these ladies were fragile, suspicious of the Army and were to be handled with kid gloves. I paused to wonder why they had assigned that task to me but relished the chance to prove myself. I initially thought the ladies to be standoffish or reserved to say the least. Gradually they thawed and relaxed to the point of being friendly and grateful for the opportunity to spend time in a city that lived life without constant terrorism. On the evening of their final day, I invited the ladies to our NAAFI for drinks. The evening went fairly well but I noticed that they were quiet. I asked the Sister in charge if all was okay. I was eighteen years old and had not been to Belfast or I would have known the answer before asking the question. The Sister told me they were dreading going back to a 'War Zone' and then said she had been on duty when Sgt Willetts was brought in. She talked us through what had happened, even though we had all read about it in the papers. As ever, the truth was painful to hear first hand. This lady was a Catholic but that did not stop her crying her heart out as she told us how sad she was that Sgt Willetts had not survived. She said she felt ashamed of her country folk. At that point, one of my colleagues put a record on the player behind the bar and we all sang along. Soldiers and nurses, Catholic and Protestant, sang along to the Harvey Andrews song and tears flowed freely down all of our faces.

The aftermath of the Springfield Road bombing.

**R.I.P  Sgt Willetts. GC**

## WPC Rosemary McGookin

## Royal Ulster Constabulary. (George Cross).

I had the honour to serve alongside Rosemary when we were both stationed at Lisburn RUC Station. Occasionally we patrolled together in an unmarked Ford Cortina car and I was immediately impressed by her compassion and professional attitude. It did me no harm to be on patrol with a beautiful young WPC as well!

There were other WPC's in the station, some of whom revelled in the attention from male colleagues. Rosemary paid it no attention. Slim, attractive, black collar length hair, Rosemary was attractive in an 'intelligent' way. I nicknamed her 'Pixie' a name she did not seem to mind. I remember on one occasion, I was Station Duty Officer and Pixie brought me a packet of Rolo's whilst I stood in the rain on guard duty outside the station. That small act of kindness touched me immensely. I looked upon Rosemary as the sister I never had. One who actually cared about other humans. On another occasion, we were called to a 'domestic' in Lisburn. The 'lady' of the house was very animated and wanted her husband removed because he was drunk, abusive and violent. Rosemary and I arrived and went in to the terraced house on a Protestant estate in the city. Rosemary talked to the wife and was told that her husband was upstairs, drunk and armed with a kitchen knife. Even though Rosemary was the senior officer, I suggested she stay and talk to the irate woman while I went upstairs to talk to the husband. Maybe I wanted to prove myself, not that I needed to to Rosemary. As I put my foot on the first stair, I heard Rosemary say, "Take care Paul, he could be dangerous." I went upstairs and the husband was sitting on the bed, knife in hand. After only a few minutes, and a heart to heart chat, which Pixie heard, we came back downstairs and the incident was over. I suggested to Rosemary that, to avoid further problems, we take the man to his own flat. She readily agreed and smiled at me in the car. After dropping off the man and advising him strongly about returning to cause more trouble, we resumed patrol. I can see Rosemary now, looking at me, smiling her beguiling smile and saying,

"Jayz but you're soft at heart Paul. We'll never make a Peeler out of ye"

I left the RUC in 1979, and shortly afterwards Rosemary was posted to Newry. When I heard about her death, I was devastated. So many people who had tried to be good citizens had been killed. So many young lives taken from us.

Rosemary McGookin's mother Mary Robinson and sister Jean McCready recall a young woman full of fun who had been married for just 20 months - sadly, they have lost touch with her husband Michael who has since re-married.

"THE pain never goes away. The heartbreak never heals. And 25 years after the IRA mortar on Newry police station - where Portadown was perhaps the most profoundly affected town in Northern Ireland - the raw memories were in focus on Sunday at the moving memorial service in First Newry Presbyterian Church."

Nine officers perished that day in February 1985, among them Portadown residents Chief Inspector Alex Donaldson (41) and WPC Rosemary McGookin (27), who were ruthlessly murdered by the mortar attack at the Frontier town police station.

The other WPC killed - Ivy Kelly (29) - had also recently moved to Portadown with her policeman husband Robert, while Constable Peter Topping also had roots in the town.

The other five officers who perished were - Reserve Constable Geoffrey Campbell (24, from Dromara), Sergeant John Dowd (31, from Lurgan), Reserve Constable Paul McFerran (33, from Belfast), Reserve Constable Sean McHenry (19, from Newtownards) and Reserve Constable Denis Price (22, from Glengormley). And there were scores of injuries.

Alex Donaldson's widow, Ida, told of a truly professional chief inspector, loving father and husband, who had promised her "a wee hug" when he returned from duty that fateful night. He never did return, and as well as Mrs Donaldson, he left three children - Samuel (then 13), Joanne (11) and Andrew (7). Poignantly, there are now five grandchildren whom Alex never saw.

Mrs Robinson - a retired nurse - said, "Never a day passes when we don't think of Rosemary and what stage in life she would have reached now. We wonder if she'd have had children, where her police career would have taken her, for she loved the RUC and had progressed into the DMSU in Newry , after starting off in headquarters in Belfast and then working in Lisburn."

Sister Jean said, "Rosemary was so full of fun. She loved driving and when she drove the police Land Rover, they used to tease her she drove too fast and their heads were hitting off the roof. She was one of three sisters - Barbara, myself and Rosemary - and we loved her so much.

"She is never out of our minds, and while Sunday's service at First Newry Presbyterian Church (on the 25th Anniversary) was a wonderful occasion, it brought it into sharp focus, especially as the dissidents' bomb last week damaged Downshire Presbyterian Church where the service was planned.

"They read out all the names of the police killed during the troubles in the Newry and Mourne area, and they were all in the RUC, and the RUC badge was the backdrop of the service.

"It still hurts RUC families the way the force was phased out - they presented them with the George Cross and then pointed the RUC towards the sunset after all their professionalism and sacrifice. That hurts so many families, especially given the fact that terrorists whose representatives carried out attacks like Newry are now in government. But that won't dim our love and happy memories of Rosemary or her real sense of fun."

Rosemary and Michael McGookin lived at Killicomaine Gardens, Portadown, and Mrs Robinson will never forget the kindness of one man who helped them through - RUC officer Ian Adair.

"It was his job to tell us and he was so sensitive and caring," she recalled. "He still keeps in touch with us and has been so compassionate over the years."

On that same night, Chief Inspector Alex Donaldson shouldn't even have been on duty. But he was there in Newry from his base at Gough Barracks in Armagh to meet controversial priest Fr Dennis Faul as part of his inquiries into a complaint and was in the canteen at the time the rockets were launched from the back of a lorry in Monaghan Street, 200 yards away.

His widow Ida, left to raise their three children, told of the last time her husband left for work and said he would give her "a wee hug" when he returned - he reckoned it would be between 6.30 and 8.30pm.

But later that night, she was visited by two police officers who broke the horrific news of the biggest loss of life suffered by the RUC during the troubles - including her deeply-loved husband.

To me, Rosemary was a wonderful person. Her life was stolen from her, her family and her friends and colleagues.

**RIP Rosemary.**

## Derek 'The Gentleman' Downey

Not to be confused with the kick boxer of the same name, Derek was a soldier then a policeman, then a Recruitment Consultant and, finally, a mature student.

Some people wear etiquette and protocol as a badge only when it suits them. The Derek I knew was a man who set great store by appearance, by manners and etiquette. He had two nicknames from we who had the pleasure to work with him. 'Snuff' after his only habit, and Mr Etiquette.

Derek Downey was born in March 1971, eighteen minutes after his twin brother, Gordon. As Derek often told me that was the only time in his life that he was ever late! He joined the British Army in 1987 as a REME Air Technician, a highly responsible position. He served several tours in Northern Ireland in Aldergrove and Ballykelly and was awarded not only the GSM (General Service Medal) but also the ASM, (Accumulated Service Medal). Derek's postings also included tours in Germany and Bosnia where he was awarded the UN Medal.

Whilst serving in Norway on exercise, Derek was carrying out a routine check on a Lynx helicopter when he found what appeared to be a minor fault. Such was his tenacity that Derek continued investigating and ultimately found a fault that, if not discovered, would have caused a catastrophic failure, which would have killed everyone on board. Such was the nature of the fault found by Derek, the helicopter was returned to Germany on the back of a low loader.

When Derek left the army, time served, he returned to Northern Ireland and joined what was then the Royal Ulster Constabulary and remained in the police when it became the Police Service for Northern Ireland, (PSNI), Derek committed himself to that role in the same way he gave his all when in the army. Derek left the REME as a Sergeant.

On one occasion as a police officer, Derek was badly injured when arresting a violent person. He was pushed through a front door window and sustained severe nerve damage to his wrist, which needed microsurgery to re-attach.

The smile we will always remember.

I had the privilege to meet Derek in Leicester. I was the manager of a Recruitment Agency and had advertised for a Recruitment Consultant. The position required knowledge of the transport industry and I was surprised when Derek applied for the job. When he telephoned, I detected something about his manner that I instantly liked.

Derek was upfront about having no recruitment experience but told me of his background in the army and police. His soft Northern Irish accent made me feel at ease and I knew he would be the ideal person. However, interviews had to be carried out and so I made an appointment for Derek to see me the following day. I discussed the candidates with Paul Mitchell, my Regional Manager and predicted that Derek would be fifteen minutes early. Paul took the bet and I was happy to be proven right. A delightful young lady who had no idea about driving had just left when the door opened and a tall, stocky man entered. His suit was cream in colour and his shirt and tie matched perfectly. This was Derek. He shook our hands and we started the interview. I noticed Paul Mitchell studying Derek carefully while I asked questions. After only a few minutes, we had all relaxed and the interview turned into a friendly chat among colleagues. I had been worrying about putting Derek at ease but it was he who put us at ease! He and I exchanged stories of the RUC and we all laughed at his tales. I explained our business and the role of a recruitment consultant and Derek chipped in with comments of his own that showed me that he had a firm grasp of what I was looking for. It was also very obvious that Derek had a high IQ and would be a great asset to my company. When I asked Derek if he had any questions to ask he only had one, one that I actually had the answer to but could not tell him at that time. He asked "When can I start?"

I had to tell him that we had other people to see and that I would be in touch. He shook our hands firmly and left. Paul and I agreed that Derek was the man but we had to see two other potentials first. Only one other candidate came close to matching our requirements. The guy had Recruitment qualifications coming out of his ears but sadly that's where his personality came from as well. Derek had outshone everyone else but there was another factor. I had been in the habit of getting my Receptionist to give me her opinion of the interviewees and Anna stated quite firmly that, if we did not appoint 'the Irish fella', we were fools! I telephoned Derek immediately and offered him the job, which, I am happy to say, he accepted. Derek started with us the following Monday, smack on time.

When Derek arrived, I had been in the office for two hours already. He politely knocked on the door and entered. His grey pin-stripe suit was immaculate and he carried over one arm an overcoat and held an umbrella in the other. One thing that Derek did that day that surprised his colleagues was to call me 'Skipper'. No one in the office knew that I had served in the RUC, albeit for only just over 2 years, so they were even more surprised when I had to explain why Derek called me that.

It was only a matter of months later that I left recruitment and started my own business as a chauffeur. I had bought a Champagne Mercedes and was very happy doing airport runs, weddings etc. Indeed, I drove Derek to the airport when he returned to Belfast on visits. My partner and her sister had met Derek many times on social occasions and were also impressed by him. Derek also decided on a change of direction and enrolled as a mature student at The University of Leicester studying Contemporary History. There he became a very popular and talented student who was committed to his work and research. He successfully applied for funding for research on the Battle of the Somme in France and Belgium. Derek also undertook voluntary work for the Stanley Burton Centre for Holocaust Studies. Derek was a keen historian with ambitions to attain a high-class degree and continue his studies with postgraduate research. Such was Derek's popularity; his fellow students elected him to the Staff-Student Committee. Derek's love of history may well have begun with his own family having a very creditable history.

Sadly, Derek was unable to attain his degree. He passed away on Monday 27th October 2008. Derek was the holder of the RUC GC General Service Medal and the Queens Golden Jubilee Medal.

Campaigns in Derek's family include the Boer War, WW1, WW2, his Grandfather being the founding father to REME, to Aden, Northern Ireland and the first Gulf War. A family, then, who are proud to serve and to do so honourably.

The Downey Family medal collection.

That smile!!!

*RIP Derek.*

# A 'Humbling' of heroes

## Major-General R E J Gerrard-Wright. CB. CBE. DL.

### 9th May 1930 – 12th May 2012.

*"I thank my God upon every remembrance of you"*

Where do I start? Well, for the purposes of brevity, and not as a sign of disrespect, I will refer to Major-General, Richard Eustace John Gerrard-Wright as "The Boss".

Richard Eustace John Gerrard-Wright was born on 9th May 1930 at Woolsthorpe-By-Belvoir, Lincolnshire. He was educated at Christ's Hospital before attending the Royal Military Academy at Sandhurst. Commissioned in 1949, he served with the 1st Battalion Royal Lincolnshire Regiment in the Suez Canal zone, and Germany and then in Malaya during the communist insurgency. During this time he was Mentioned in Despatches.

The Royal Lincolns were amalgamated with the Northamptonshire Regiment to form 2nd Battalion East (later Royal) Anglian Regiment and, after returning to Sandhurst as an instructor, he served with the Poachers in Germany. In 1963, after passing the Staff College examination, he attended the Indian Defence Services Staff College in south India.

The Boss became Brigade Major of the 70th (East African) Brigade in Kenya during which time he sat in on cabinet meetings chaired by Jomo Kenyatta. For his role he was appointed MBE. In 1966, The Boss moved to Malaysia as Brigade Major of the 28th (Commonwealth) Brigade. Whilst in Malaya in the 50's, The Boss adopted a pet monkey, called Psmith, whom he promoted to Lance Corporal. Maybe that is one reason why he and I got on so well! The monkey was soon reduced to the ranks when, on one occasion, it lost it's temper, climbing to the top of a tent he sprinkled it's occupants with talcum powder. The Boss's sense of humour was legendary even back then and I was to learn that as well as a deep sense of fun, he was an extremely shrewd people manager. In 1970, The Boss took command of the Royal Anglian Regiment and served two tours of Northern Ireland, which quickly established him as a first-rate battalion commander.

One story he told me was that, when being shot at, he reported the 'contact' over the radio. The Ops Commander asked if the shots were high or low velocity. The Boss's reply was typical.

"I have no idea" he reported, "But the bullet was going bloody fast when it passed me!"

He was promoted from Lt Colonel to Brigadier in an accelerated promotion. General Frank Kitson once said to him "there are boots men, and there are shoes men in the army, and you are a boots man" . This meant that he was better in the command of men than in an office job in the Ministry of Defence, which was a compliment from Sir Frank Kitson!

At the end of this tour, he was again Mentioned in Despatches and appointed OBE. The Boss was obviously due a rest and held a staff appointment at HQ 1 BR Corps in Germany but soon returned to Northern Ireland as Brigade Commander of 39 Infantry

Brigade. In 1977, he was advanced to CBE and left Lisburn for the Canadian National Defence College in Ontario. In 1979, The Boss returned to HQ 1BR Corps as Chief of Staff. Promotion to Major-General followed the year later upon becoming GOC Eastern District. After a spell at MOD as Director TA and Cadets, in 1985, The Boss was appointed CB on retiring from the Army. Some career!

I met 'The Boss' in early 1975 when he came to Lisburn as Brigade Commander 39 Infantry Brigade. My crew, Rover Group, and I were apprehensive at the arrival of the new Brigadier, The reason being that the outgoing Brigade Commander was a dour Scot who barely tolerated his driver and escorts. The day came and we met our new boss outside the HQ building at Thiepval Barracks, Lisburn. The officer who strode confidently towards was perhaps 6 feet tall, immaculately cut dark hair and had a very military moustache. We saluted and he introduced himself. Whilst I introduced his new crew, he shook hands with each of us and asked questions about our past and what we did in the crew. I sensed an immediate rapport building with The Boss and relaxed. We had a good one here!! I ventured to ask his PA, Penny, her opinion.

"Oh you had better be on your toes, Cpl," she said, "This one is a live wire!" She was right.

'The Boss' in his office at 39 Inf Bde. Lisburn.

The rest of the crew went back to our building, Rover Group, and Lofty Newman and I went to the Brigadiers Married Quarter to meet the rest of his family. Boxes were being unpacked and the house had the look of organised chaos. Sue, the Brigadiers lovely wife, was busy supervising but took the time to greet us. Lance and Rufus, two lively but well behaved young lads were helping. The Brigadier had two daughters, Rosie and Philipa but we did not meet them on that occasion.

The next few weeks flew by. The Brigade held a conference three days a week at different locations in Belfast and it was my job to find out where. We would assemble outside HQ and wait. This Brigadier was punctual to say the least. He was also very personable, what I would call a soldiers officer. One day, The Boss discovered that he was entitled to use a helicopter to travel around Belfast. That seemed to put our jobs in jeopardy and so we set about protecting ourselves. Conference was to be held in Girdwood Park in Belfast and, when the 'chopper' took off, so did we! We shot out of the gate, blue light flashing and two-tone horns blaring. When The Boss landed at Girdwood Park we were there waiting for him, coffee and egg banjo's in hand. The look on his face was a picture!

"How the hell did you get here before me Corporal?" he asked.

"I put my foot down for a change, Sir" I replied. He rarely used the chopper again!

If there was an incident, a bomb, a shooting, tarring and feathering, The Boss wanted to be there. On one occasion, a senior clergyman had been assaulted in his own home and we visited. The Boss went inside without his bodyguard, not something that happened often. He sincerely apologised to the cleric, made him tea and chatted for quite some time. Given that the clergyman was a Catholic, this impressed him immensely. The Boss had the knack of making everyone feel comfortable, no matter colour, religion, race or rank. This knack set him aside from most officers, or Ruperts as they were known, affectionately!

The Boss made many friends on both sides of the divide in Northern Ireland. His honesty, courtesy, co-operation and strength of character impressed nearly everybody he met.

It was never a dull moment with the Brigadier. Even going out in the civvy car with him was interesting.

Another aspect of the job was to take Sue and her daughters shopping in Belfast. I remember we fought over that job!! It would occasionally be myself and a Royal Pioneer Corps escort, in civilian clothing, normally suits and armed, however his batman, Cpl Hayes, usually made this trip. We took that job particularly seriously, parking the car in Grand Central Hotel, an army post, and walking through the shops. Getting into shops was sometimes a problem as the security would want to pat us down. We had to hold our ID cards in the palm of our hands, discreetly.

The Brigadier decided that he needed to give up smoking and booked a session with a hypnotist. Half an hour later, he emerged, despondent. It seems the hypnotist could not put him under as his mind was too active. I can believe that.

In 1976, Sir Kenneth Newman was appointed Chief Constable of the Royal Ulster Constabulary, (RUC) and the Brigadier 'volunteered' a couple of us from Rover Group to give him a guided tour of Belfast. Sir Kenneth flew into Lisburn by helicopter and we set off in our 'spare' Landrover Safari, one that did not have blue lights but did contain two-tone sirens. We spent the next three hours driving through all areas of the city, liasing with the local units so that we were not caught up in any incidents. The nearest Sir Kenneth came to action was when we drove through Ballymurphy at a crawl. A few bricks hit the 'rover, then a pot of paint and I had seen enough. Sir Kenneth held tight as I flew through the streets, scattering the few yobs. I then prayed he did not mention it to the Boss!!

Eventually, the two years that The Boss would spend in Lisburn came to an end. My own time in the army was soon to be up and I was honoured when The Boss asked me to stay on and be his driver at his next posting. I discussed this with my, then, wife but she was not keen. In the end I made the wrong choice and left the army to join the Royal Ulster Constabulary.

The night of the Brigadiers farewell party arrived and I collected him from his quarter and drove him to the Horseshoe Club, 39 Brigades own pub in camp. We had had a portrait painted and proudly presented it to him. The Boss was visibly moved and very pleased. All evening he drank with us, the rest of 39 Brigade who were in the club must have been green! When it was time for him to go home, he insisted that I not drive him, he would take the staff car and I would collect it next morning.

Leaving party for 'The Boss' and the portrait presented to him.

His 'Crew' bidding this very popular officer, Farewell.

It is now 2016 when I am writing this. It was in 2014 that I learned of The Boss's passing away. I was devastated. I contacted other members of Rover Group and let them know. I then did some research on the internet. I read how, one evening in 1996, The Boss and Sue were waiting at a taxi rank in London when a children's nurse struck The Boss in the face after he had suggested that she take her place in the queue. His glasses were smashed and he was injured in one eye. At the court case, the nurse accused The Boss of racial abuse. The Boss strongly denied this and I would support him 100%. There was not a racist thought in The Boss's mind. The judge saw through this nurse, telling her that she had used the "race card" to escape the results of her own actions. She was sentenced to 12 months imprisonment but this was reduced on appeal.

After the army, The Boss and Sue settled in Lincolnshire where he helped to establish the Royal Lincolns regimental collection in the Museum of Lincolnshire.

Lincoln Cathedral hosted a Service of Thanksgiving to celebrate the life of Major-General Richard Eustace John Gerrard-Wright CB, CBE, DL on Monday 10th September 2012 at 2.30 pm.

Her Majesty's Lord-Lieutenant attended, as did a host of serving and retired soldiers and officers, family, friends and colleagues.

An extract from the Service guide reads

"Dick will be remembered for his huge sense of fun, his love of music, his lasting concern for his soldiers and his devotion to the county – but mostly as a devoted husband, father and grandfather"

True words indeed.

I have always had the greatest of respect both for The Boss and Sue. John Kelly, Lofty Newman and I all agree. He was the only officer in the British Army that we would have gladly died for.

*RIP Sir.*

Monday, 10th September, 2012
2.30 pm

Some of the Brigadiers Crew. 1976

A long hot summer!!!

The 'Belfast Lean'.

## Brigadier Richard Dawnay, OBE

August 1975. Belfast.

The three quarter ton Landrover Long Wheel Base drove fast up Durham Street towards Unity Flats. 'Rent a mob' were enjoying one of their daily riots. Suddenly the landrover screeched to a halt and my back up 'Rover nearly rear ended it!

I grabbed the microphone and radioed forward, "9 this is 45, is the road blocked? Over"

Yobs, mostly dressed in Bay City Roller style clothes, mostly short Tartan trousers, pelted the vehicle with bricks, bottles of paint and other assorted missiles. The reply was quick and terse,

"45, this in 9, our driver has frozen over!"

I did not have time to think, the rioters were getting braver, I shouted over the noise of missiles hitting the macrolon of the vehicles,

"Escorts, baton rounds, dismount!"

I jumped from my seat and, as John and Norman joined me, gave orders.

"Nige has frozen, fire baton rounds into the mob. I'll get him out and into the back of the escort vehicle and take over the Colonels 'Rover. John, you drive the escort and we'll get the hell out of here."

John and Norman fired at the mob while I ran to the driver's side of the Colonels 'Rover. Pulling open the door I saw 'Big' Nige staring ahead, hands gripping the steering wheel. I prised his hands away and pulled him hard out of the seat and ran him to the back of the escort vehicle, where Sid, the Radio Operator, stood, also firing baton rounds at the crowd who screamed insults and lobbed bricks. Once Nige was inside, I ran back to the lead vehicle and jumped in. Two loud beeps of the horn saw John and Norm run back to their own vehicle and climb aboard.

I turned to look at The Deputy Commander, 39 Infantry Brigade. He sat smiling, extremely calm, his Browning 9mm pistol in his lap.

"Good evening Corporal" he said, smiling.

"Good evening Sir" I replied, "Where to Sir?"

He simply pointed straight ahead, into the mob and towards Brown Square RUC Station.

I radioed the backup vehicle,

"Lock tight 45, we're moving off, straight ahead!"

The Deputy Commanders vehicle was fitted with a blue light and two-tone horns. I switched all of these on as well as the headlights on main beam and hazard lights. I hoped this would distract the rioters and was lucky. As I accelerated fast forward, they parted and we made rapid progress to the Police Station, albeit still under attack. On entering the station car park, it was difficult to park up due to the amount of vehicles already there. I made a 98 point turn, much to the Colonels' amusement.

"Thank you Cpl, " he chuckled. "I think you are now my driver, is that OK?"

"Well, someone has to do it, Sir!" I replied.

He dug his hand into his combat smock pocket, brought out a five pound note and said,

"Get the crew egg banjo's and coffees, Cpl, we'll need all the energy we can get tonight!"

And, so began my time driving Colonel Richard Dawnay, OBE, Parachute Regiment.

August 1975. Taken shortly before the rioting kicked off by Unity Flats, Belfast.

Colonel Dawnay can be seen crossing the road to talk to the 'local' troops.

Richard Dawnay was born on 20th April 1930. He was educate at Sherborne School in Dorset and was commissioned into the British Army as a 2nd Lt in July 1950. He joined the Parachute Regiment in May 1958.

In the early sixties, he was Deputy Adjutant and Quartermaster General of 44 Independent Para Brigade and then Officer Commanding D Company, 1 Para. After being promoted to Lt Colonel, he commanded 2 Para from 1968 to 1971. As Officer Commanding 2 Para, Richard Dawnay became the Commander of a force inserted into Anguilla to quell civil unrest. He received the OBE for his actions on this operation. The citation for the award records:

"Lt Colonel Richard William Dawnay landed in Anguilla on 19th March 1969 with the spearhead of Force Anguilla. This force, which he commanded, consisted of part of 2nd Battalion The Parachute Regiment, a half squadron of Royal Engineers, elements of the Royal Army Medical Corps and the Royal Corps of Signals and a detachment of the Metropolitan Police.

Contrary to expectations, the landing was unopposed but the reception given to Lt Colonel Dawnay's troops by the majority of the Anguillan people was derisive and, in many instances, openly hostile. The soldiers and policemen ignored this provocation and, emboldened by the disciplined behaviour and friendly attitude of the Force as a whole, the public endeavoured to take advantage of the situation by organising and participating in aggressive demonstrations against the established authority.

Had this situation been permitted to continue, a state of general disorder would have prevailed on the island but the Force Commander maintained complete control of the situation throughout this difficult period. In fact Lt Colonel Dawnay commanded his Force with exceptional skill and restraint and, as a direct result of his leadership and grasp of the situation, the action taken by the security forces never exceeded routine Internal Security measures and, consequently, Anguilla was occupied and held without bloodshed.

This important achievement not only restored law and order in Anguilla but, eventually, it won the respect and co-operation of the people, and this paved the way for the introduction of an effective civil administration. As the situation improved, Lt Colonel Dawnay consolidated his early gains by concentrating the efforts of his troops on winning the hearts and minds of the Anguillan people. In this he was also successful, with the result that the problem of establishing and maintaining a stable administration of the island was considerably reduced."

So, taken as a whole, the Parachute Regiment won hearts and minds, without bloodshed, whilst restoring law and order. Some might say that that is not the reputation of the Para's that most people hear about!

Following the operation, 2 Para were awarded the prestigious Wilkinson Sword of Peace. Not mentioned in the media these days!

After a tour as Liaison Officer at Fort Benning in the USA, Richard Dawnay became GSO1 for Airborne and Special Forces HQ in UK Land Forces.

He received a Mention in Despatches for services in Northern Ireland in 1975. Following his departure as Deputy Commander 39 Infantry Brigade in Lisburn, Northern Ireland, Richard Dawnay was promoted to Brigadier and became Director of Army Recruitment in 1979 and retired from the Army on 10th April 1983.

During his time in Northern Ireland, Dawnay threw himself into the role of Deputy Commander with a gusto. His crew were on 20 minutes stand by at all times and I alternated between him and the Brigade Commander, seven days a week. Lisburn is often referred to as 'Slipper city', a reference to the more relaxed atmosphere for soldiers stationed in Thiepval Barracks. However, not all those serving there had it easy. Rover Group, the unit containing the Brigade Commanders and Deputy Commanders Crew were often hard pushed to keep up. Sleep came whenever and wherever it could and, if an incident had happened anywhere in the Belfast area, we would be attending with one or other of these Senior Officers. In effect we were very much left alone by the HQNI, Headquarters Northern Ireland. We wore our own style of uniform, often Para smocks and trousers, rarely wore the 'flak jacket', which we saw as totally useless. Rover Group was often ridiculed but never to our faces!

When it came time for Richard Dawnay to say farewell to Northern Ireland, Rover Group chipped in and bought him a statue of a bronze stallion and had a plaque engraved. Sadly, the engraver misspelt his name, much to my embarrassment! We invited the Colonel, as he then was, to Rover Group to have a farewell drink. His surprise at the presentation was total and I remember we all had wet eyes as he made his short speech. Over the two years we had worked with him, Colonel Richard Dawnay had been an excellent officer and Deputy Commander. I still have a reference that he had typed up for me and used it in civilian life for a long time. When I returned to England, Richard and I wrote to each other and I also went to London to visit him in his role as Director of Army Recruitment. Having tea in the Savoy with a Brigadier was, for a mere Corporal, something of an achievement.

**Thank you Sir.**

## "Felix"

Who are Felix?

Felix is the unofficial mascot of the British Army counter-terrorism bomb disposal. Maybe because cats have long been associated with good luck, well, they always seem to land on their feet. Felix is Latin for 'happy' or 'lucky' and was the name of a popular cartoon cat in early 1900s America. Cheerful, thoughtful and seemed to survive unscathed. Many bomb squads worldwide adopted the cat as their symbol.

SSgt Brian Shepherd when serving in Northern Ireland in the 1970s originally drew the Felix used by the British Army. There is a story that a young signaller was sent to the Commanding Officer 321 EOD to ask which call-sign the unit wished to use. The OC, having lost two operators that day, suggested 'Phoenix, to suggest the Squadron was rising from the ashes. The signaller misheard him and used 'Felix' and this has never changed.

"Fetch Felix"

Bomb Disposal is, arguably, the most dangerous job in the British Army. Hundreds of lives were saved in Ulster by the actions of these extremely brave men and women.

Sadly, the cost has been high. Between 1969 and 1973, seven bomb disposal officers lost their lives in Northern Ireland.

The first officer to die in Northern Ireland was blown up by a sophisticated anti-handling bomb placed outside an Orange Hall at Castlerobin, near Belfast on September 9th 1971. Terrorists placed the bomb in the bottom of a wooden box. Once spotted, the bomb disposal officer was called and decided to move the device, believing it to be an ordinary device. As he moved the box, very gingerly no doubt, a micro-switch was operated and the bomb blew up, in his face.

In Lurgan, a bomb disposal officer entered a shop to look for the device and it exploded.

Quite often, if a bomb was discovered, the bomb disposal officers would leave it for some time to see what would happen. However, they could not leave it forever and needed to move in to disarm it or carry out a controlled explosion.

During my time in Belfast, I watched many bombs being made safe. I also saw many explode before they could be dealt with. Watching the officer making the 'long walk' towards an unexploded bomb was chilling to say the least.

Royal Avenue. Belfast.

Ammunition Technicians are currently employed by the Royal Logistics Corps, (RLC) formerly the Royal Army Ordnance Corps. (RAOC) and have become highly proficient in bomb disposal, most of the experience having been gained after many years operating in Northern Ireland. Bombs used by PIRA (Provisional Irish Republican Army) ranged from simple pipe bombs to very sophisticated victim-triggered bombs with infra-red switches. Roadside bombs, commonly used in Afghanistan today were used in Northern Ireland in the early 70s. Mortars were also used by PIRA, normally in stationary vehicles. Between 1969 and 2007, 23 British bomb disposal operatives were killed in action in Ulster.

312 EOD was formed specifically to combat increased IRA violence. Targets ranged from military to economic and were totally indiscriminate. These terrorists had no respect for human life. The IRA seemed hell bent on killing bomb disposal officers and became more devious as time went on.

321 Coy RAOC is the most decorated unit, in peace time, in the British Army, with over 200 Gallantry awards, most for bravery during Operation Banner.

Today's bomb disposal unit, 11 EOD Regiment RLC, were specifically requested by the US Marine Corps to assist in clearing Iraqi oilfields of booby traps and were amongst the very first British service personnel sent into Iraq in 2003. Before the actual invasion!

The training ATO's receive is quite extraordinary. As well as conventional and homemade bombs, they are trained in chemical, biological, incendiary, radiological and nuclear bombs. They provide assistance to civilian authorities and train personnel from all three services. They are still in operation in Northern Ireland, despite the PSNI (Police Service Northern Ireland) having their own trained operators. RLC

Bomb Disposal Squads are nearly always called out in Northern Ireland. I will not state my opinion on this!

The course training ATO's is some three years long and is not only extensive, it is gruelling.

I salute these brave men and women. Without them, in Northern Ireland in particular, many more lives would have been lost.

**Thank you!**

## Troggs!

### (aka, The Royal Corps of Transport)

**"Victory is the beautiful, bright-coloured flower. Transport is the stem without which it could never have blossomed."**

Sir Winston Churchill, KG, OM, CH

What, or who, is a Trogg? Opinions differ, indeed, some ex RCT had never heard the expression until it was mentioned on Facebook a few years ago! My belief is that the expression comes from Troglodyte, a being that never leaves its cave. Ergo, drivers never leave their cabs!

The RCT has a main task. To manage, control and operate all means of transport by land, sea and air for the movement and distribution of men and material for the British Army, wherever it may be.

When I joined, in 1971, Intake 262, the RCT was still fairly new, having been formed on 15th July 1965. I had taken one driving lesson in 'civvy' street, aged 17. I told my instructor that I intended joining up, he advised the RCT, being an ex RASC man himself. The RASC, Royal Army Service Corps, was our predecessor.

Our history goes back as far as 1415 when a 'Baggage-Sergeant' was appointed and then, in 1422, a 'Master of the Baggage Train' was appointed. On arrival at Buller Barracks, Aldershot, I was met by the RSM, Regimental Sergeant Major. This was not planned however! On the parade square was a rehearsal for a Passing Out Parade and so I skirted 'Gods Little Acre' with care. Unfortunately, another new recruit did not and strolled onto the square and tapped the RSM on the shoulder!

"scuse me mate" he asked, "I'm new here, where do I go?"

The RSM, who, if I remember was called Mustard, went purple in the face and bellowed,

"To the effing Guardroom! You two men, fall out and escort this man there!!"

We never saw the new recruit again!

I stood and watched the parade for a while, battered suitcase by my side, not knowing where the hell to go. The RSM saw me and marched in my direction. As he approached, I drew myself to what I imagined attention was. He actually smiled!

"Good morning Sir," I said, "I am a new recruit, where do I report?" A right creep!!!

He led me to the main office and handed me over to a Corporal Evans.

"Taff" he said, "Look after this young man will you?"

I was dead impressed that I had made a good impression! Not for long though as a Sgt came in.

"Fucking creep!" he snarled. "Get rid of him Cpl Evans!"

That Sgt made my life a misery during my basic training. Nothing I did was right, every thing I did was wrong. A bit like my last partner!!!

I survived basic and moved on to driver training. I failed my first test but passed the second time. Next day I started HGV 3 training and, after one and a half days, took my test. The examiner took me from Aldershot to Farnborough then told me to return. I spent the trip wondering how I had failed. On arrival at Buller Barracks, he told me I had passed! Stunned, I asked why we had not done the full test. His response was that he had a date that night with a hot chick and he needed to get ready!! His other comment made me proud though.

"You went through some gaps that I would not have attempted. You obviously know what you are doing."

Every new recruit, no matter what Corps or Regiment, has a built in pride in their Unit. I have said for many a year that Squaddie humour is the best in the world. Trogg humour is the best of the best! Troggs the world over have been able to smile, if not laugh out loud, at the most macabre things. I guess I fitted in quite well!

As I have written before, this is not meant to be a comprehensive history of the RCT. Better men than I have done that. In fact, if you want a really honest picture of the RCT, buy 'Rickshaws, Camels and Taxi's' or 'Harry was a Crap Hat' by Harry Clacy. I have never met him but I have read his books and 'chatted' on Messenger. His books bring the RCT back to life for me and I read them often. Thanks Harry!

In brief then, our predecessors were The Commissary-General, famous for being at Rorkes Drift, The Corps of Waggoners, the Royal Waggon Corps and the Royal Waggon Train. Not to mention the Army Service Corps, the Royal Army Service Corps followed by our good selves, the Royal Corps of Transport, now known as the Royal Logistics Corps, or Really Large Corps!

The Royal Army Service Corps was redesignated The Royal Corps of Transport on the 15th July 1965 and would include the Transportation elements and Movement Control Service of the Corps of Royal Engineers to become the Army's Transport and Distributive Corps. At the same time its responsibility for providing rations, forage, fuel and petroleum products, together with its Barracks and Fire Service elements and its military Staff clerks were transferred to its sister Corps, the R.A.O.C, or 'blanket stackers' as we called them.

The colours of the Royal Corps of Transport include the blue and white of the RASC and its predecessors, together with the red, traditional to the Royal Engineers and thus remind the officers and soldiers of the new Corps and its proud past. 29 members of the Royal Corps of Transport lost their lives during Op Banner. RIP every one of them.

The Royal Corps of Transport was lost in 5th April 1993 and is now the Royal Logistics Corps. Nicknamed the 'Loggies' or 'Really Large Corps', the RLC was formed by the union of five Corps, The Royal Engineers, RCT, Royal Army Ordnance Corps, Royal Pioneer Corps and the Army Catering Corps. Both regular and reserve units were included. The RLC battle honours are, Peninsula, Battle of Waterloo, Lucknow, Taku Forts and Peking.

I am proud to have served in the RCT. My brother was a Snowdrop, RAF Police and I had no intention of following his footsteps! I have some standards! (Low they may be, but standards all the same!)

Anyway, where was I? Oh yes, our history. The RCT, by any name, has provided transport and logistics to other units through two World wars, The Crimea, the South African War, The Gulf War, Iraq and Afghanistan not to mention Northern Ireland, where Troggs not just drove vehicles on the streets but they took part in patrols. Sport played a very important role in the RCT life. In particular, 10 Regt in Germany, hosted the best boxing team ever in the British Army, defeating the Para's on occasion! We worked hard, played hard, fought hard and, of course, drank hard! Troggs became known as extreme drinkers before the expression was thought of. There are many trades in the RCT, in all arms of the Army. I was, lucky? to be chosen as a Staff Car Driver, driving Senior Officers. Many of whom I grew to know personally and to respect. (See previous Chapters). In my time in the RCT, I attained the dizzy heights of Corporal but could, maybe, have risen higher. I often wonder how my life would have turned out if I had not chosen the RCT. Boring, I suspect. The Sgt who gave me such a hard time in Basic was called Sgt Bob Card. He was Para qualified and an extremely fit bloke. I met him again in Moscow Camp, Belfast, a few years later. He bought me a pint and said he was glad I had persevered with Army life and he was not sorry for making my life a misery as it made me the man who sat before him. Until that night, I had hated him! But, sat in the choggie I realised just how much I owed him. Thanks Bob.

I believe that Bob Card became RSM of 10 Reg. Takes one very hard man to do that!!!

*Regimental Police in Regents Park Barracks, London*

*Belfast in the 70's*

Between driver training and being posted to London, I was nominated as driver to the Officer Commanding, 12 Training Regiment, RCT. This was a Major Nicholas. He reminded me of Colonel Blimp! He had joined the RASC during National Service and risen through the ranks. I admired that. I drove him for nearly six months. Little did I know but we would meet up some 35 years later when I ended up living with his eldest daughter! He knew of my RCT past but, up until now, I never let on that we had met previously, let alone that I was the driver he hated most! Ooops, cat out of the bag now then!

Being a Staff car Driver in London was exciting. I became the personal driver to the Chief of Staff, London District and took over the evening he received a letter bomb that took off his left thumb and three fingers from the same hand. I had just arrived at his flat of Brompton Road and saw him open the letter. It gave me a hell of a shock but called 999 and the emergency services quickly took over. When he came out of hospital, I was given a different car every day to drive him and an RMP Bodyguard. We were in civvies and in a civvy car. The Brigadier decided to retire and it was back to uniform to drive the new Boss. This Brigadier had been Brigade Commander in Londonderry during the Bloody Sunday marches in 1972. He and I often chatted in the car on his way home and he told me a lot. I now wish I had taken notes! I saw on Part One Orders one evening that I was to be posted. To Lisburn as Brigade Commanders Driver. The Chief of Staff offered to get it cancelled but I said no, that had been my destination and I would go there.

Being in London had shown me to be a hard worker but, as I guess with most Troggs, a hard drinker too. Getting into trouble came too easily to me, and it was probably for the best that I went to Northern Ireland.

I ended up in Lisburn after a nightmare journey on the ferry from Liverpool to Belfast. Drunken squaddies vomiting everywhere made it a very uncomfortable journey for all on board. The next day I stood on the deck watching Belfast getting closer, expecting to hear bombs and shots everywhere. Nothing. Nada!! Peaceful and quiet. I was met by an RCT Movements Corporal in uniform but with a civvy jacket in the plain white coach. He had a Browning 9mm pistol and that was it! Our security. After about an hour, we arrived at Thiepval Barracks and unloaded ourselves. It did not take me long to settle in. Initially I drove Bedford RL trucks, to acclimatise myself to the area. We were given a lecture on the situation in Northern Ireland, issued our Blue and Yellow Cards, our personal weapons and sectarian maps. Green for Catholic areas and Orange for Protestant areas. How I got to drive the senior officers is detailed in previous chapters. During my time in Lisburn, I saw bombs, shootings, and riots and did patrols in Belfast. On my first patrol in the city centre, I was crouched in a doorway when a young woman passed my. Her son, maybe four years old, saw me and I said, "Hi". His response was one I would hear a lot over the next five years, "Feck off ye Brit Bastard!" I was taken aback, especially when the mother said, "Welcome tae Belfast"!

Also during my time in Lisburn I met and married my first wife, Ann, and we had a son, Simon. He was born in the Lagan Valley Hospital in Lisburn. When I went to visit, I did so in uniform. A security guard tried to relieve me of my SLR, (Self Loading Rifle) but realised that he was unable to whilst pinned to the floor! My wife left hospital that same day, maybe 48 hours earlier than necessary! Ann and I moved into a married quarter inside Thiepval Barracks. Being married gave me more freedom to move around Lisburn and I did not let up on my duties. Looking back, I gave the army more of myself than I put into my marriage. That said, it lasted 13 years! Married pads stuck together and, every three months or so, a group of us would go out, get drunk and let our hair down. It was our way of letting off steam. Many a time, on our way home, we would be seen performing on the dog assault course, even lighting the flaming circle and diving through it!! By and large, our wives were remarkably tolerant.

Whilst in Rover Group, the Brigade Commanders Crew saw, dotted around Belfast, various small orange signs, placed by local units. The Para's were in the shape of a parachute etc. Rover Group decided not to be outdone and got our heads together. We decided that, as Northern Ireland had a plentiful supply of rain, our emblem would be a Wellington boot! See below.

A competition was launched. Each member of Rover Group would try to place this sticky backed 'Wellie' in the most daring places. The highest, the most obvious, the riskiest and the most dangerous. Loads of sticky back 'Day-Glo' was obtained, either scrounged or indeed stolen! A rubber stamp was made and, on off duty moments or when bored, we all sat cutting out 'wellies' by the hundred! It became more than a sport, more of an obsession! The winner of the most outrageous placement went to our RMP Bodyguard, Spud, who managed to secure one to the meeting room table in Stormont when the 'Boss' was in a meeting with Ian Paisley. I won the highest when, flying back to Belfast from Birmingham, managed to secure a large 'wellie' to the cockpit door of the airplane. The most obvious went to a person not to be named who, on a raid on an illegal club on the Falls Road, Belfast, secured one behind the bar as we left. I am told it took them weeks to spot it! Lofty Newman and I met up whilst on leave and drove to Wellington in Somerset and literally plastered the place with them! Lofty was a great mate, a L/Cpl RCT on the crew, who had a wicked sense of humour and was a legend on the dance floor in the NAAFI! All of our landrovers had at least one wellie on it. However, I claim the most dangerous wellie placing. After a few weeks of our magic wellies appearing everywhere, the RSM (Regimental Sergeant Major) started receiving complaints. It was a Friday morning and I was flying home on leave. As I passed the Squadron offices, the RSM 'called' me in. More like a bellow that could have been heard in Manchester! As I walked towards his office, my comrades shrank back, thinking I was in deep doo-doo!! I knocked on his door and entered, standing at attention in front of him. He calmly informed me that he knew we were responsible for the outbreak of 'wellie measles' and that I was the ringleader. I kept schtum! He delivered his bollocking whilst pacing around the office; occasionally stopping to gaze out of the window before informing me that 'wellie' posting would stop. Immediately. I nodded, said "Thank you Sir" and left his office. My taxi was just leaving the main gate when I saw the RSM running towards me, shaking his Pace Stick in the air and pointing at the wellie I had placed on it while he wasn't looking! I made it to the airport without incident, went on leave and returned to camp two weeks later. The RSM had been posted to Germany as Master Driver and I was safe. Needless to say, we carried on posting 'wellies' until I left the army. The picture above is of a wellie that I sent to a famous actress. I met her years later and she returned it, as she thought it was the only one left. Bless her, no names, no pack drill. I have often thought about starting the 'wellie measles' craze again!!!

I worked with some incredible characters in the RCT, too many to mention them all but a few stand out for a variety of reasons. Jock McGee in London. Short, fiery, difficult to understand, Jock would sometimes steal an army car and go for a drive. I attended his wedding to a WRAC (Women's Royal Army Corps) and was nearly arrested for being caught in an compromising position with a girl I was dating! Whilst home on leave in Coventry, the IRA attempted to blow up the telephone exchange but only succeeded in killing themselves, what we called 'an own goal'. I heard the explosion from my house and new instantly what it was. I lived in Radford and we had many Irish neighbours, none of whom liked having a soldier in the same street. In London, I had left the Central London Recruiting Depot just minutes before a car bomb exploded there. Now, in Belfast, I had seen plenty of minor scales of action. The RCT were attached to every unit serving in Northern Ireland between 1969 and 2007. Many lived in horrendous conditions, in old mills, old police stations, even old schools. They were cramped, often cold and wet but the Troggs soldiered on. It is said that the British Squaddie sense of humour is the best in the world. In that case, Trogg humour is the best of the best!

John Kelly, Cpl, RCT in Lisburn is probably the most outstanding memory. One night in the NAAFI, when John was Canteen Cowboy, the NCO in charge of the disco, John and I had a competition to see who had the biggest nose! I won! By a nose, you could say! I met up with him again in July 2010 and it was just like 32 years had not come between us! When my partner, my son and I arrived at Johns house, we were treated like Royalty by John and his lovely wife, Kathleen. We were 'in country' for a week and spent a fantastic day, reminiscing and laughing. Plenty of photographs were taken, my son, Daniel, totally adored John and Kathleen and the feeling was mutual. My, then, partner, had not understood just how much comradeship means in the armed forces, despite her father having been a Major in the RCT. John knows that, if ever he needs me, I will be there, and vice versa. Thanks John, I will be back mate!

A professional driver and soldier, John and I were like chalk and cheese. I loved going on the road with him. On one occasion, with Brigadier Gerrard-Wright, whenever the Boss looked to his left, I would smack John on his ear with a baton! John would yelp and the Boss would ask what was the matter. John could not say, however and we in the back would be wetting ourselves with laughter! Sorry John. Our RMP Bodyguard was a manic-depressive who was learning the chanter, part of bagpipes. He drove us mad with his efforts. God he was awful! On one occasion, he threw the escorts SLR's on the road because he did not want them in the 'rover. I wonder what happened to Pete? He was so bad that, on another occasion, a record he had bought jumped on the record player. Pete threw the player and record out of his window in the camp and then proceeded to kick it around the Parade Square, whilst wearing his best-bulled boots! Even the RSM walked in a different direction on seeing this!

In Lisburn, there was a young Royal Pioneer Corps Private who would sit in the NAAFI from 11 am to 11 pm, day in day out. He drank. And drank. And then drank some more. This was 'Billy'. The only time he left his seat was to go to the bar or the toilet. He had a bucket beside him into which he threw up with startling accuracy. The NAAFI girls would remove the bucket, empty and clean it before replacing it. The story I was told was that 'Billy' had had a particularly bad tour a couple of years previously and, on being told his posting back to the Province, refused to soldier. Such was the family attitude of his colleagues and officers; 'Billy' came to Lisburn but did no work whatsoever. In that way, he could be posted away after his two years with a clean record. I have no idea if 'Billy' actually survived his tour. I hope so.

Whilst on route back from Belfast to Lisburn one day in 1976, we heard on the radio that there had been a shooting in Belfast and the suspect car, a dark blue BMW, had joined the M1 motorway and was possibly behind us. We set up a VCP, (Vehicle Check Point) across the two-lane motorway and waited while cars passed through. Finally, a blue BMW approached and we pointed to the driver to move off the carriageway. I had been a Lance Corporal for about a year by then and was eager for promotion. Inside the car were four men, all dirty, scruffy and unshaven. We surrounded the car and ordered them out. As they lay on the embankment, I searched the car. Car? More like a mobile arsenal! There were shotguns, machine guns, pistols and grenades inside. I could see my second stripe being stitched on!! The radio op called Lisburn on a secure channel, gave them the details and we waited. I walked across to the men and nudged one in his foot. "Name!" I demanded.

A very English voice said, "Wait until your Ops Commander calls you back son!"

My second stripe disappeared before my eyes and was replaced with a bollocking that I would get on return to camp. Eventually, Zero called back and told us to get rid of them.

I walked back to the scruffy blokes and knelt down, whispering, "I've been told to get rid of you, how should I do it?"

He said, "Grab me by the neck, pick us up and tell us loudly to fuck off!" It turned out they were SAS and were not involved in the incident reported. A couple of nights later, sat in a pub in Lisburn, a pint of lager appeared on my table. I looked around and there were the four SAS guys, smiling at me.

"Well done mate," he said, and with that they walked out. I think my heart stopped for a few seconds until I relaxed. Strangely enough, thirty years later, whilst living in Greece, I was approached by a Geordie lad, similar age to myself. He brought with him a pint of lager. He smiled and said, "That's twice I've bought you a pint mate!" It was one of the four SAS guys from the M1 incident. I spent the next two years chatting to him. Sadly, a drunken Greek that we both knew killed him in a drink drive accident. Sad end to a great life. I had left Greece by then and was mortified.


I enjoyed my time in the RCT immensely. Would I do it again? Damn right I would. Would I let my son join the RLC? Maybe, just maybe.

The Warrenpoint massacre, or Narrow Water massacre, was carried out by the PIRA. South Armagh Brigade on 27th August 1979.

Terrorists ambushed the British Army with two large roadside bombs at Narrow Water Castle, near Warrenpoint, at the border with the Republic of Ireland.

The first bomb was aimed at an army convoy and the second targeted reinforcements sent to deal with the incident.

I do not intend to go too deeply into this outrage. That has been done elsewhere, by more qualified writers than I.

However, at approximately 16.40 on the 27th August 1979, a convoy of one landrover and two four-ton lorries was driving past Narrow Water Castle on the A2. A 500 lb bomb, hidden in a lorry parked near the castle, was detonated by remote control. The first lorry was flung onto its side, killing six members of the 2nd Battalion Parachute Regiment instantly. Their bodies were scattered across the road. Only two soldiers in that lorry survived, both had serious injuries.

Immediately the bomb blew up, the soldiers believed they were under attack from sniper fire from across the border, approx 50 metres away. They returned fire and, an uninvolved civilian was killed by this gunfire. Michael Hudson, a coachman at Buckingham Palace, and his cousin, Barry Hudson, was wounded. They had been innocent bird watchers on an island opposite the castle.

At approx 17.12, some thirty-two minutes after the first explosion, a second bomb hidden in milk pails exploded against the gate lodge on the opposite side of the road. The IRA had been paying close attention to how we behaved after a bomb incident and correctly guessed that an ICP, Incident Control Point, would be set up by the lodge. The second bomb was a bigger one than the first, being some 800 lbs. This device killed twelve soldiers, ten from the Parachute Regiment and two from the Queens Own Highlanders.

A press photographer, Peter Molloy, came very close to being shot by an angry Paratrooper who saw him taking photos of the dead and dying instead of helping the wounded. The soldier was tackled by his comrades. Molloy states that 'I was shouted at and called all sorts of things but I understood why. I had trespassed on the worst day of these fellas' lives and taken pictures of it'.

Two 'men' were arrested after the bombings, Brendan Burns and Joe Brennan but they were later released on bail due to lack of evidence. They had been stopped by Irish police while riding a motorbike on a road near Narrow Water Castle. Brendan Burns was killed in 1988 when a bomb he was transporting exploded prematurely. He was an IRA member. Joe Brennan, also an IRA member, was jailed in 1982 for carrying out an armed bank robbery to raise funds for the IRA. He is alleged to have left the IRA in 1986 and went on to become a successful property developer and novelist. I make no comment!


The Warrenpoint Massacre occurred on the same day that Lord Louis Mountbatten was killed by an IRA unit near Sligo, along with three others.

Many other incidents occurred in Northern Ireland between 1969 and 2007. Captain Robert Nairac, abducted, tortured and murdered, the two innocent Corporals, abducted, tortured and murdered and many, many more. The British Army was ordered onto the streets to restore law and order. They made every effort to do so; often sleeping (when sleep was possible) in horrendous conditions that migrants to this country would riot over. Under fire, under attack, under pressure and under paid.

When I served across the water, I received a massive 50p per day, 'danger money'. Oh and a medal. The GSM, General Service Medal, with Northern Ireland clasp. I also received the ACSM, Accumulated Service Medal and a GSM for serving in the RUC, Royal Ulster Constabulary. I served in the police for less than two years. I came back to England because I realised I just was no good at the job. My abilities failed to match my ambitions. But I was there, I walked the walk and now, to some people's annoyance, I talk the talk. We veterans must stick together because the Government will allow others to shaft us at every opportunity.

## The Corporals Killings

On the 19th March 1988 I was the Manager of a bakery supply company and was based in Bodmin, Cornwall. On that fateful day, my wife and I had checked into a hotel in Newquay in preparation for a Dinner Dance that evening. On entering our room, I turned the television on and was horrified at what I saw. My wife had to leave the room, it was so shocking. I will take those disgraceful images to my grave.

### Background.

On the 6th of March 1988, three IRA members preparing for a bomb attack on the Band of the Royal Anglians in Gibraltar, were killed by members of the SAS (Special Air Service). The funerals of these terrorists were unpoliced at Milltown Cemetery, Belfast. UDA (Ulster Defence Association) member Michael Stone, attacked these funerals with pistols and hand grenades. Three people were killed and more than sixty injured. One of the dead was Kevin Brady who was an IRA member. Brady's funeral, just three days later, took place amid a fearful and tense atmosphere. IRA members acted as stewards.

*

Cpl David Howes and Cpl Derek Wood were serving soldiers in the Royal Corps of Signals, based in Lisburn, Northern Ireland. On March 19th 1988, they drove into Belfast in a silver VW Passat. They were wearing civilian clothing and Cpl Derek Wood was armed with a pistol. It is presumed that the Corporals drove into the area by accident. My opinion is that they were simply getting to know the area and had not realised that a funeral was taking place in the area.

The Corporals somehow managed to arrive in the Andersontown Road where the funeral procession was moving towards Milltown Cemetery, preceded by several black taxis. Reports say that the Corporals car headed straight towards the procession, driving past an IRA steward who tried to flag the car down. The mourners say they believed they were under a Loyalist attack. The Corporals car turned into a side street but this road was blocked. The car reversed at some speed and ended up within the funeral cortege. Cpl Wood tried to drive away but black taxis blocked his path. 'Mourners' surrounded the car, windows were smashed and the 'mourners' tried to drag the Corporals out. Cpl Wood drew his pistol, waved it in the air and fired one shot into the air, not aiming at anyone. I watched as the crowd raced away only to return with even more ferocity than before. Several of the mob had weapons, which they had snatched from photographers. The car was pummelled and after a few minutes, the Corporals were dragged from the vehicle. The world saw these men being kicked and punched to the ground. They were then dragged to Casement Park, not far away, where they were again beaten and stripped to their underpants and socks by a small group of 'men'. Their clothes were searched and showed that the men were not a Loyalist hit squad but soldiers. A Catholic Priest, Father Alec Reid, tried to stop the assault and begged for an ambulance to be called. However, he was dragged away and told if he did not move on he would be shot. The Corporals received another beating and were thrown over a wall and bundled into a taxi. The cab raced away and a fist can be seen punching the air.

Just about 200 yards away was Penny Lane, just off the Andersontown Road and the taxi stopped here. The Corporals were dragged out, thrown to the ground and shot. Cpl Wood was shot six times, twice in the head and four times in the chest. He had also been stabbed four times in his back.

Father Alec Reid had followed the taxi and gave the Corporals the Last Rites. A photographer, David Cairns, took a photo of Father Reid kneeling beside Cpl Howes. The photo is iconic and horrifying.

The IRA then had the audacity to release a 'statement'. In it, the Belfast Brigade claimed responsibility for the execution of two 'SAS members', who, the IRA claimed, launched an attack on the funeral cortege. Sick, demented ego's these IRA have.

Two 'men', Alex Murphy and Harry Maguire were found guilty of killing the Corporals. In 1989, they were both jailed for life with a recommendation they serve at least 25 years. Murphy received a further 83 years and Maguire 79 years for bodily harm, false imprisonment and possessing a gun and ammunition. Obviously, in 1998, only ten years into their sentence, the two were released under the Good Friday early prisoner release scheme.

Both were senior IRA members. Murphy, aged 15, had been the youngest republican internee in Long Kesh in 1973. Maguire also spent time in The Maze, as Long Kesh became known and he was one of the prisoners to meet Mo Mowlem when she visited to negotiate with prisoners.

The chief Steward on the day of the funeral, Terence Clarke, was sentenced to seven years in prison for assaulting Cpl Wood. Clarke had previously been bodyguard to Gerry Adams.

I switched off the television and opened the mini bar. Sitting on the floor of a hotel room, glass of whiskey in hand, my mind went over what I had seen. I cannot say how angry, disgusted and totally saddened I felt. Even though, at the time, the identity of the Corporals was not known, any veteran of 'The Troubles' would have realised what they were. Right at that moment, I hated everything Ulster! Trying to put this out of my mind for a few hours, I joined the melee in the Dinner Dance. Then a colleague introduced me to his wife. She spoke with a soft voice, in a Northern Irish accent and I was rude.

"Catholic or Protestant?" I asked.

My colleague looked embarrassed as she replied, "Protestant Paul, and I know why you ask. It wasn't my lot who killed those two poor soldiers today".

Like a deflated balloon, I let out a loud sigh of relief. She and I sat for a long time, outside the main event, talking about Ulster. I think I told her things my own wife did not hear from my lips. Eventually, my colleague claimed his wife and my wife claimed me. I appreciated that chat.

This has been the hardest chapter for me to write. This incident had such an impact on me and for every soldier who served in Northern Ireland. When I hear these murderers labelled dissidents, political prisoners or, as one woman called them 'freedom fighters' I want to scream. They are murderers, pure and simple. I make no apology for my sentiments or how I see them.


R.I.P. Corporal David Howes and Corporal Derek Wood.

We will never forget.

A 'Humbling' of heroes

## UK VETERANS-ONE VOICE

Uk veterans-One Voice is a Facebook group started in 2015 by veteran Nigel Kelsall. The aim of the group, initially, was to show support for L/Cpl J, a Parachute Regiment Veteran who had been questioned in respect of his alleged involvement in the Bloody Sunday incident, in Londonderry in 1972. Veterans across the UK were incensed at this arrest by the Police Service Northern Ireland. (PSNI) Nigel realised that something had to be done and so he started the group and enlisted the help of, at that time, hundreds of members. Initially, emails were sent to MP's asking for their input to stop the injustice. Only 17 replied. They all said the same thing. "We cannot interfere with the rule of law". In other words, they could interfere when they gave 'Get out of Jail Free' letters to convicted terrorists but had no intention of helping British soldiers who, at the end of the day, were simply doing what the Government at the time wanted. Within eight days, yes, just eight days, Nigel had organised a march in London to present a petition to David Cameron, Prime Minister. The petition contained almost 25,000 signatures. Some achievement. But Nigel did not stop there, nor did his team of Admins. The pressure was stepped up and, when another group organising a march for January 5th 2016 stepped down, Nigel and his team took over the group and, within a mere six days, had organised yet another march! Media coverage for the first march was poor. The BBC did not want to know. The only TV coverage was on Russian Television! However, the march was reported in newspapers in other countries and Nigel was not disheartened. Approximately 300 ex Forces Veterans paraded and marched to Downing Street. They held two minutes silence at the Cenotaph. The January march however was much more widely publicised. Forces TV, part of the British Forces Broadcasting Service (BFBS) sent a reporter and film crew and the march was shown on Forces TV news programmes. The newspapers soon became involved, with the Daily Mail doing a feature on the protest and even The Sun gave us a mention! Over 100 ex Forces Veterans paraded and, again, respectfully held two minutes silence, to remember the fallen. Remember, this was on the first Monday of 2016 and not many people could get the time off to attend at such short notice. By this time, the protest was not just for L/Cpl J. It had emerged that soldiers who had served in Iraq were being investigated for crimes. That was bad enough but the ambulance chasing lawyers were using taxpayers' money to provide Legal Aid for those Iraqi's making a claim. It gets worse! Jeremy Corbyn, leader of the Labour Party, had appointed Emily Thornberry as his new Shadow Defence Secretary. Ms Thornberry is alleged to have received some £48,000 from a firm of lawyers to help her career in politics. Now then, you would think this was all bad enough. No. The same firm of lawyers are alleged to have withheld vital records that could have stopped an inquiry into the claims, thereby saving millions of taxpayers' money! They are also alleged to have destroyed a vital piece of information. At the time of writing, a firm of lawyers are facing a disciplinary hearing after the Solicitors Regulation Authority found the firm had failed to establish if Iraqis they were representing were insurgents or villagers. You could not make this up except there is a final twist in the tale. A firm of lawyers have been paying an Iraqi agent nearly £40,000 per year to recruit and help the families of so-called victims! These are some of the reason why Nigel and his team are organising more protests. And all this is on a voluntary basis. No one receives a penny from anyone for all his or her hard work and dedication. The group are also campaigning for the release of Sgt Blackman, the Royal Marine jailed for killing an Iraqi insurgent. That case is subject to appeal. I joined the group at the beginning and was proud when Nigel asked me to join his team. Between two groups, Veterans March and UK Veterans-One Voice, they now have close to 20,000 members, all seeking justice. This is not something that the British Government can ignore any longer. At the time of writing, we have marches planned for the 20th February 2016 in London, Manchester, Cardiff, Edinburgh, Leeds, Exeter, Portsmouth and Nottingham. My son, Daniel, will be marching beside me and will be one of the team presenting our petition to David Cameron at Downing Street. We have a strong team of Admins who keep the group in line especially Lynne, our 'Pin-up' girl! Neil is our Internet genius and all the others work very hard to keep the momentum going. I am proud to be associated with Nigel and his team. This is not over yet. #onevoice!!!

We made the papers! Front-page news on some.

Nigel, being interviewed for Forces TV at the second march in London, January 2016.

Nigel Kelsall, Founder of

UK Veterans-One Voice, at The Cenotaph. 2015.

My son, Daniel, showing

his support. 2016.

# A 'Humbling' of heroes

On a personal note.

The Good Friday Agreement allowed hundreds of terrorists to be released from prison. It also allowed many more to escape punishment for their terrorists' activities. At the same time, Veterans and being hunted down and persecuted for doing their duty. This is not right. I do not believe that soldiers should be above the law. I do believe however that ambulance chasing lawyers and their 'spurious' claims are wrong. Stop them from using taxpayer's money to 'recruit' claimants. Our pressure forced David Cameron to 'declare war on spurious claims'. Whether he will succeed is another question. Now the Government hatchet people are talking of prosecuting soldiers for murder whilst serving in Iraq. This is an absolute disgrace! Terrorists becoming Ministers? Veterans being persecuted? Tell me, just what sort of country do we now live in? I for one am sick of it. I am not alone.

Serving in Northern Ireland in the 70's has had a profound effect on me. I still sit facing the door if I ever go out. I can still walk backwards! I am still aware of my surroundings, of people around me and those who may be a threat. I walk checking rooftops and windows, not because I am paranoid but it is inbuilt in me, even at the ripe old age of 62! I find it difficult to listen to 'The British Soldier' by Harvey Andrews without getting emotional. I feel the same listening to 'Nairac GC'. Especially when played by the Guards Bands.

I have only touched lightly on the subject of Northern Ireland. If you wish to read more, any book written by Ken Wharton, such as 'Sir, they're taking the kids indoors' will open your eyes to what really happened. Ken has written many books on the subject and is, in my opinion, a supreme authority on the subject.

This book is my tribute to people I have met and served with, or I have read about or been told about.

To all the people I have met, heard about or read about that helped inspire my life, I say thank you. To Sue Gerrard-Wright and her family, my heartfelt gratitude for permission to pay a tribute to Major-General REJ Gerrard-Wright. CB, CBE, DL.

A man amongst men. To those who gave their lives in Northern Ireland, all of Ulster owes you their respect and a massive debt of gratitude. I do not know if a true 'peace' is even possible in Northern Ireland. I hope so. I met some wonderful people over there.

Thank you for reading.

Paul Rees.

A 'Humbling' of heroes

"When we've said Goodbye"

By Paul Rees.


Read an excerpt from the debut novel by Paul Rees.


Silver grey mists, swirling in front of his eyes, much like cigarette smoke under a ceiling fan. No sounds heard, no emotions felt, no pain suffered. Limbo, somewhere between life and death, a strange sensation, neither hot nor cold, neither breathing nor dead. A time without time.

*Am I dreaming? What happened to the barbeque? Where the hell am I? I am lying in a hospital bed; harsh bright white light is forcing me back into the mattress. Pinning me down. Why are there soldiers around? I see them, armed to the teeth, facing away from me. Protecting me? From what? Or from who? All is silent in this place of safety. No one moves not even the soldiers. A memory floods my mind and I wonder why it is me who is in hospital, not Les. We had an argument about who was to be 'tail end Charlie' on our patrol. I outranked Les but he wanted his turn at being the last man to form our 'brick' of four. The argument was heated and, in the end, I had backed down. Our patrol was late leaving the base at Springfield Road Police Station and the CO was giving us grief. We 'hard targeted' through the gates of Springfield Road police station and ran flat out for the first three hundred yards. So far so good. Twenty minutes later, we turned off the Falls Road and into Percy Street. A new Security Interface had been built and it was down to us to check it was still in one piece. I went first, Caesar (Norman Hobson) second, Legs (Keith Diamond) third and then Les. Only one streetlight shone and I raced through its ambient glow. Caesar and Legs followed swiftly but Les hung back for a few seconds too long. Then, as if he felt he had a point to make to me, he ambled through the glow of the lamp and a shot*

*rang out. Les went down as if pole axed, which I suppose he was. Legs and I opened*

*fire in the only direction a shot could have come from, peppering a brick wall fifty*

*yards away until our mags were empty. Then Caesar emptied his twenty rounds in the*

*same direction while I dragged Les into cover behind a builders skip. Legs called*

*'contact' over the radio and we took up defensives, waiting for the Saracen*

*Ambulance to reach us. Silence fell until, five minutes later; we heard the scream of*

*gears as the Saracen driver roared into the street. We all piled in, lifting Les carefully*

*but the medic told us it was too late. Les had gone.*

*One shot through the head. One-shot Willie had struck again. Because I lost a verbal*

*argument with him. Les was dead because of me. Was that why I was in the hospital?*

*I glance to my left. Les is there. He should have been a film star, not a Military*

*Policeman. Dark hair, almost cherubic face, physique that Arnie would have died for.*

*He looked at me, eyes closed, face pale. I heard him say, 'it wasn't your fault, Pav'*

*yet it was and I will never, ever forgive myself for what happened. It should have been*

*me! The soldiers disappear and doctors in their pristine white coats take their place.*

*They look down at me, faces sombre. Have I died? Their lips move but I hear no*

*sound. I cannot move. My sight swivels left but my eyes are closed. Les has gone too.*

*Maybe now would be a good time to panic?*

"When we've said Goodbye" is available on Amazon.